musings for a mellow mood

Jacquie Hoffman

Eastwood Publishing Co., Denver, Colorado

MUSINGS
FOR
A
MELLOW
MOOD

*Copyright © 1979 by Jacquie Hoffman
All rights reserved. Printed in U.S.A.*

*No part of this publication may be
reproduced or transmitted in any form
or by any means, electronic or mechanical,
including photocopy, recording or any
information storage and retrieval system
now known or to be invented, without
permission in writing from the publisher,
except by a reviewer who wishes to quote
brief passages in connection with a
review written for inclusion in a magazine,
newspaper or broadcast.*

Designed by Jacquie Hoffman

*Quotation from COMPLETE POETRY AND
SELECTED PROSE OF JOHN DONNE
reprinted by courtesy of Random House, Inc.*

*Quotation from INDIA'S LOVE LYRICS by
Laurence Hope reprinted by courtesy of
Dodd, Mead and Company, Inc.*

*Quotation from MOUNT ANALOGUE, by
Rene Daumal, translated by Roger Shattuck.
Copyright © 1959 by Vincent Stuart, Ltd.
Reprinted by permission of Pantheon
Books, a Division of Random House, Inc.*

*Quotation from THE PROPHET, by
Kahill Gibran, reprinted with permission
of the publisher, Alfred A. Knopf, Inc.
Copyright © 1923 by Kahill Gibran and
renewed 1951 by Administrators C.T.A. of
Kahill Gibran Estate, and Mary G. Gibran.*

*to my husband who
encouraged me, my
children who humored
me, and my lawyer
who challenged me,*

my deepest gratitude

*the graphic interpretations
found in this volume were
created by david southern
in honor of his family*

contents

wistfully yours   *1*

naturally   *15*

truly yours   *27*

imminently yours   *41*

really yours   *55*

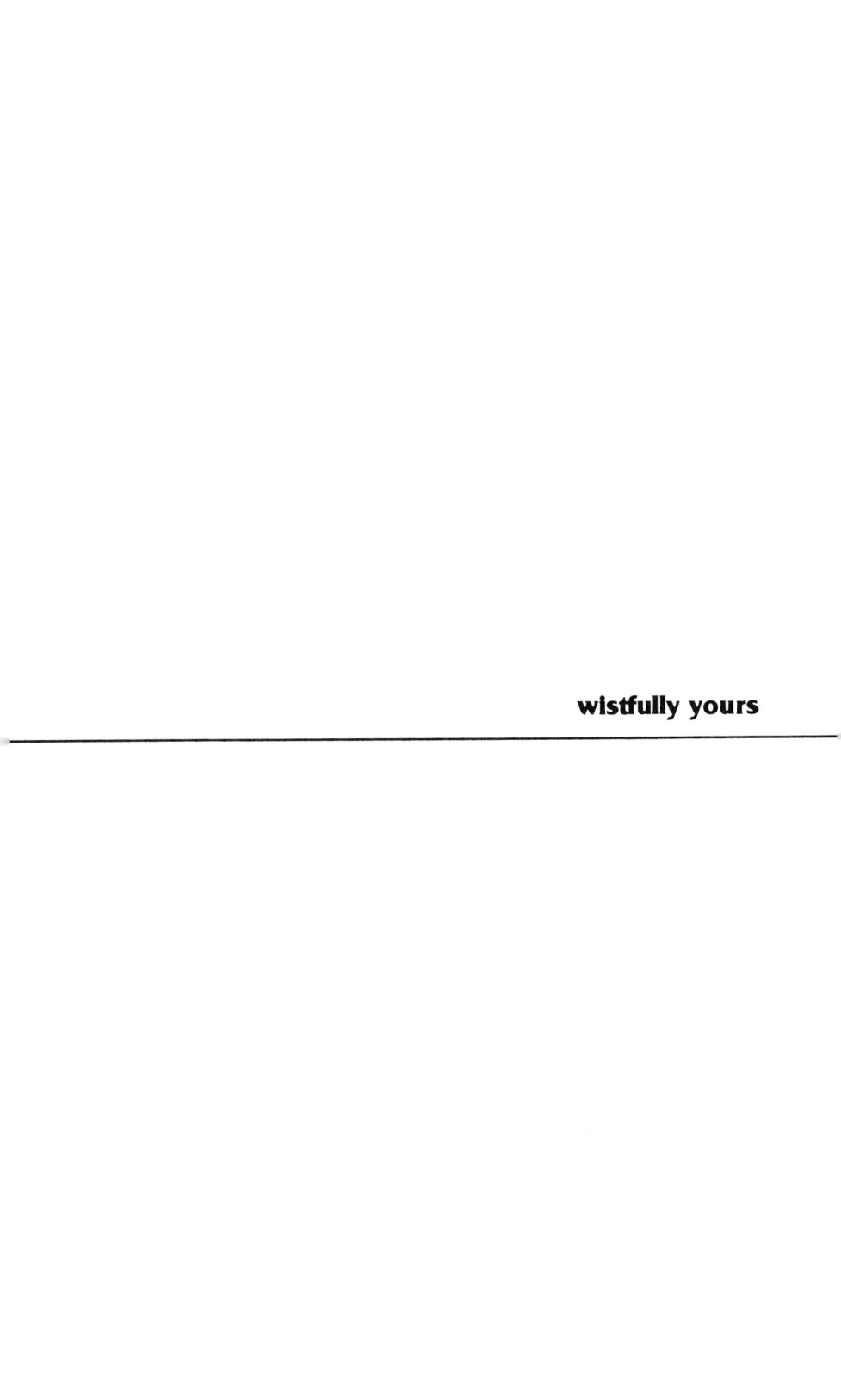

wistfully yours

holding
with a touch of velvet
searching
curiously

feeling
with a blithe spirit
giving
tenderly

loving
with a singing heart
needing
willingly

parting
with lingering footsteps

* * * *

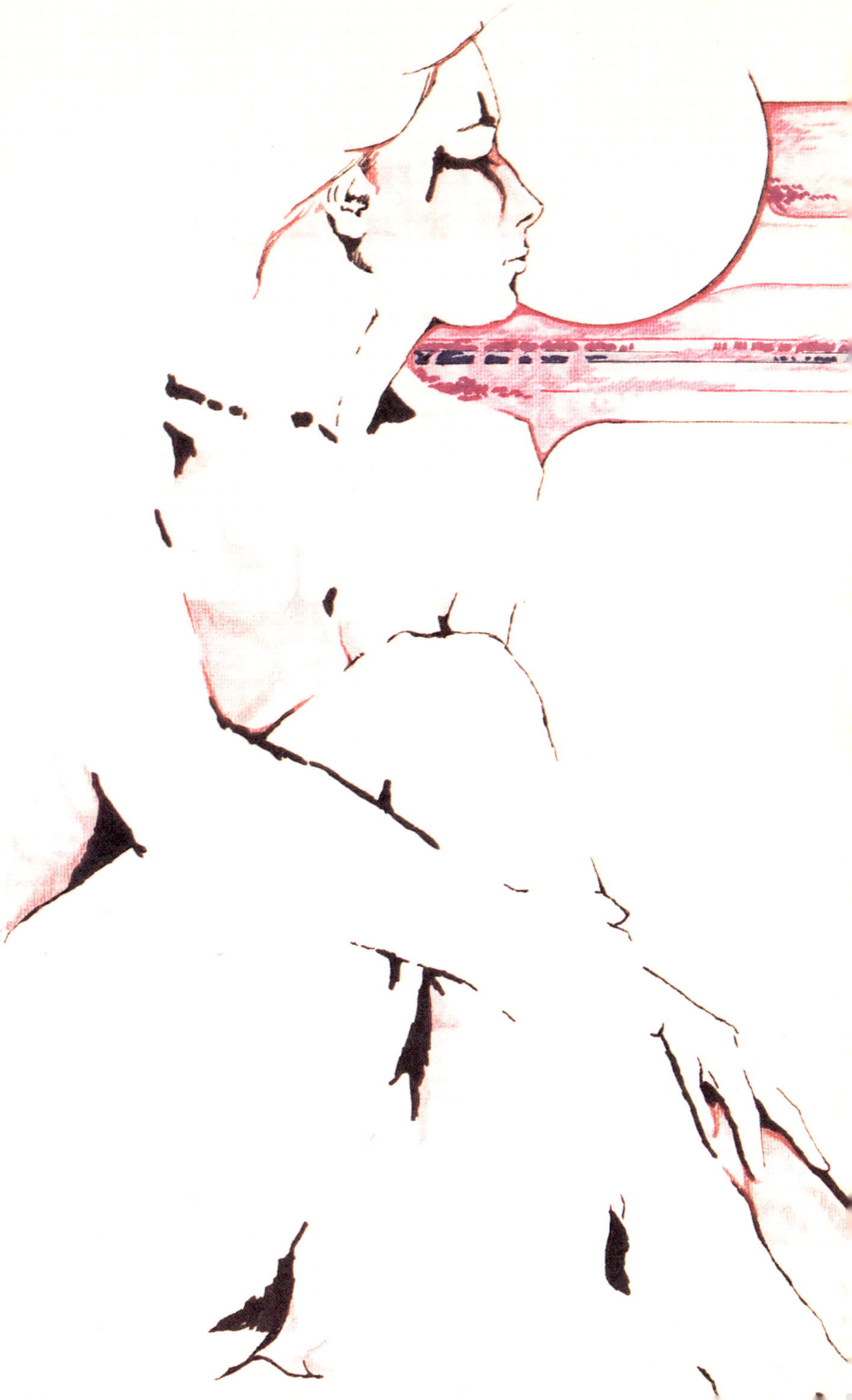

if you pull up my roots
  are you responsible for me

                * * * *

if I can stop one heart from breaking
  I shall not live in vain
if I can ease one life the aching
  or cool one pain
or help one fainting robin
  unto his nest again
I shall not live in vain

                emily dickinson

suffer in satin

                * * * *

*how do I love thee? let me count
   the ways.
I love thee to the depth and breadth
   and height
my soul can reach, when feeling out
   of sight
for the ends of being and ideal
   grace.
I love thee to the level of
   everyday's
most quiet need, by sun and
   candle-light.
I love thee freely, as men strive
   for right;
I love thee purely, as they turn
   from praise.
I love thee with the passion put
   to use
in my old griefs, and with my
   childhood's faith.
I love thee with a love I seemed
   to lose
with my lost saints, – I love thee
   with the breath,
smiles, tears, of all my life! –
   and, if God choose,
I shall but love thee better after death.*

*elizabeth
barrett
browning*

feelings
  flowing freely
    realities
      looming forcefully
      gently enhancing and enriching
        each other
          harmoniously

             * * * *

if I become what you want
who will I be then

* * * *

if you have found me
why do I feel lost

* * * *

I am dead because I lack desire
I lack desire
because I think I possess
I think I possess
because I do not try to give
in trying to give
you see that you have nothing
seeing you have nothing
you try to give of yourself
trying to give of yourself
you see that you are nothing
seeing you are nothing
you desire to become
in desiring to become
you begin to live

rene daumal

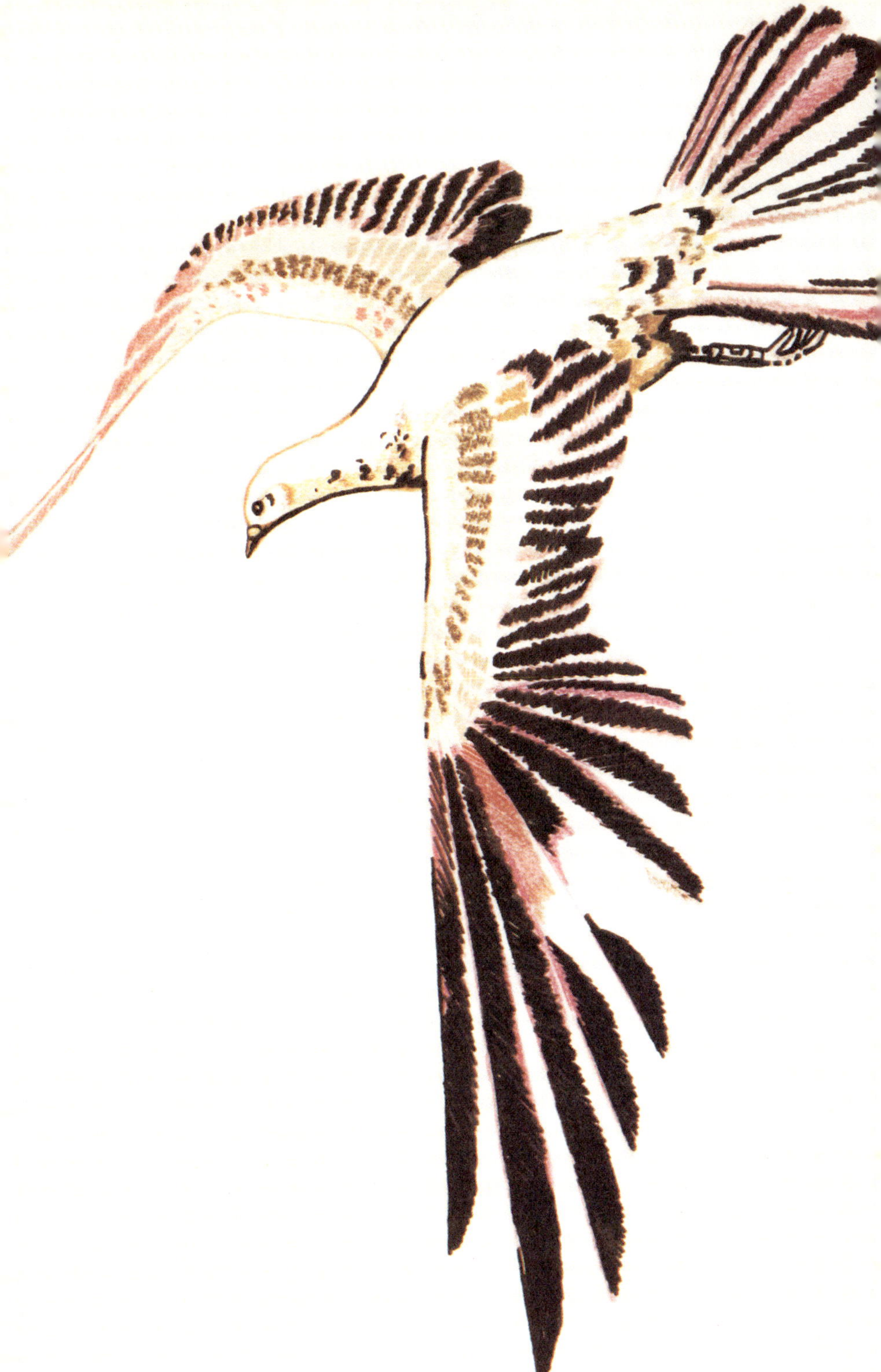

*love is envisioning
   another person's dream*

     * * * *

*when you touch me
   I feel warm all over
when you hold me
   I feel safe
when you kiss me
   I feel surrender
when you come to me
   I feel communion*

     * * * *

*away from your glow
   I feel cold*

     * * * *

in this cold cruel world
  everyone needs a warm body

    * * * *

sandy beaches
  and trade winds
    tousled hair
      and two straws
        and all our tomorrows
          together

    * * * *

everyone should come
  from a back rubbing family

    * * * *

give me beauty in the
  inward manner
    and may the inward and
      outward be one

                               plato

I see the twilight in your eyes,
  and my heart fills
with a longing, and yearning, and aching,
  for the years of your nurturing.
you are the essence of my being;
  for without you
I am nothing; a drifting shell,
  set apart, empty and alone.
you are my inspiration; for
  without you I am hopeless.
you are my self-esteem; for
  without you I am worthless.
you are all of my reserves, my resources;
  my reservoir,
inherently.

* * * *

naturally

the peace of a drifting sky
 the spirit of dancing raindrops
the courage of a crocus all alone
 in the snow
the inspiration of celestial infinity
 the hope of a sprout
the freedom of a gentle breeze and
 the innocence of falling snow are
  the elusive quests of man

for natures force is life's momentum

* * * *

*strive for that certain dignity
of a snow capped mountain*

* * * *

*may the road rise to meet you
may the wind be always at your
back
may the sun shine warm upon your
face
and the rains fall soft upon your
fields
and until we meet again
may God hold you in the palm
of his hand*

unknown

*all the wonders
and mysteries
of nature
are glorified
in a blossoming rose*

* * * *

moderation
has never been practiced
by nature

* * * *

the drifting cloud
and infinitely blue sky
give pace to our existence

* * * *

natures
predictable
cycles
generate
continued hope
in human beings

* * * *

all things are changing

marcus
aurelius

he who has his head
   in the clouds
      risks stubbing his toe

      * * * *

we must not hope to be mowers
  and to gather the ripe gold ears
unless we have first been sowers
  and watered the furrows with tears

it is not just as we take it
  this mystical world of ours
life's field will yield as we make it
  a harvest of thorns or of flowers

                johann
                wolfgang
                van goethe

man
  like the turtle
goes nowhere
   until he sticks his
     neck out

                unknown

*love one another, but make not a
   bond of love;
let it rather be a moving sea
   between the shores of your souls.
fill each other's cup but drink not
   from one cup.
give one another of your bread but
   eat not from the same loaf.
sing and dance together and be
   joyous, but let each one of you
   be alone,
even as the strings of a lute are
   alone though they quiver with the
   same music.*

*give your hearts, but not into each
   other's keeping.
for only the hand of Life can contain
   your hearts.
and stand together yet not too near
   together;
for the pillars of the temple stand
   apart,
and the oak tree and the cypress grow
   not in each other shadow.*

kahil gibran

into each life
   some rain must fall
     some days must be dark
        and dreary

                    longfellow

we must walk beyond the horizon
  one day at a time
    one step at a time
      ultimately

          * * * *

oh, but a man's reach
  should exceed his grasp
    or what's a heaven for

                    robert
                    browning

hope springs eternal
  from the human breast

                    alexander pope

serenity
 is the silence
  of falling snowflakes

        * * * *

no man is an island, entire of itself;
 every man is a piece of the
continent, a part of the main; if a
 clod be washed away by the sea, a
promontory were as well as if a manor
 of thy friends or of thine own were;
any man's death diminishes me, because
 I am involved in mankind; and therefore
never send to know for whom the bell
 tolls; it tolls for thee.

john donne

color gives the world dimension

        * * * *

as naturally
 as one season ends
 and another begins
  people pass in and out of
   your life.

all of these impressions or
 omissions
 form the essence of you.

* * * *

truly yours

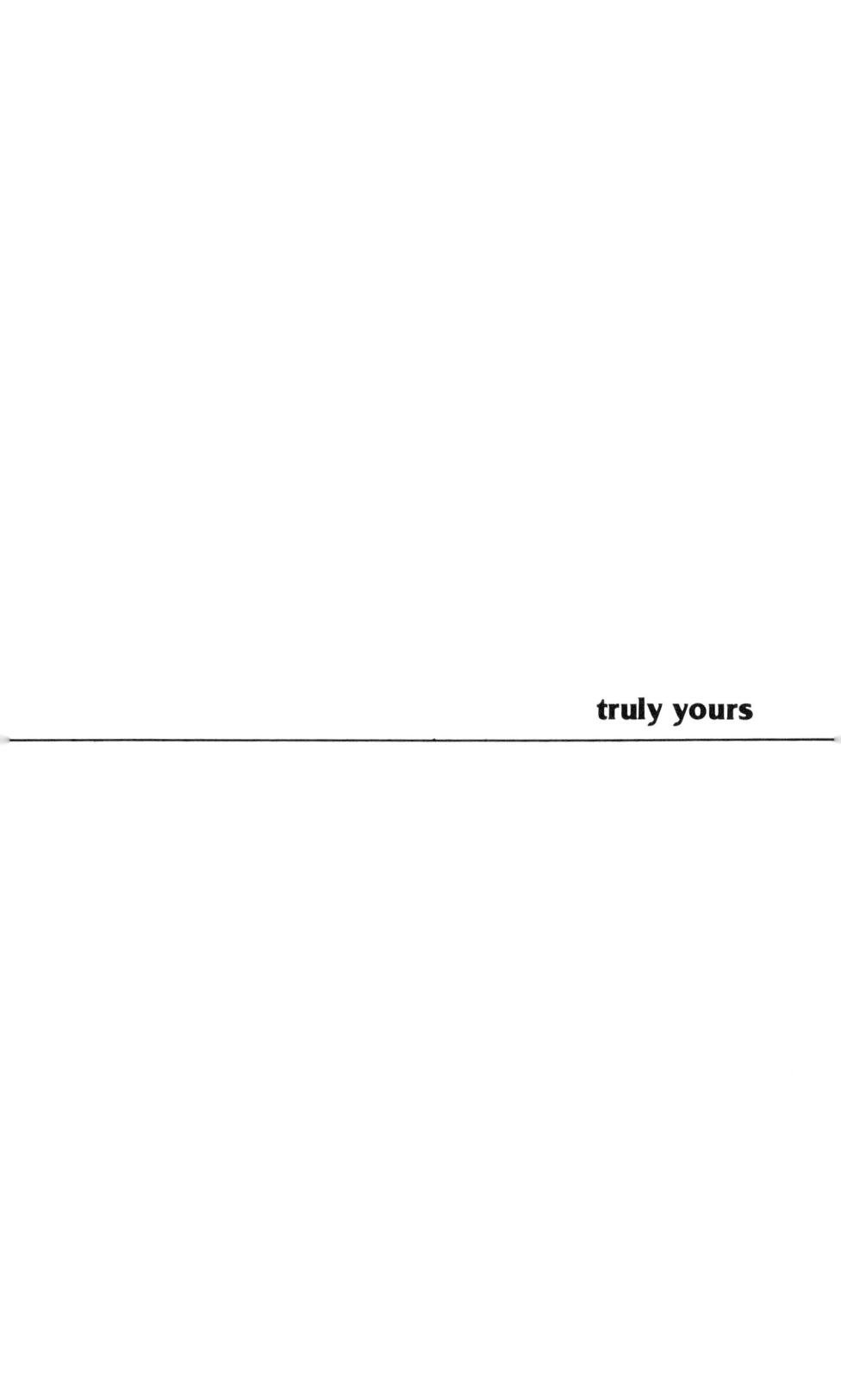

find yourself

*open   charming   observant
   gracious   tranquil
sympathetic   warm   curious
   fulfilled   attentive
loyal   humble   trusting
   optomistic   humorous
perceptive   growing   shy
   industrious   loving
patient   giving   interesting
   principled   exciting
tender   understanding   active
   tolerant   organized
eager   dignified   natural
   self-assured   spontaneous*

* * * *

*if a man does not keep pace with his
   companions, perhaps it is because
he hears a different drummer. let
   him step to the music which he hears,
however measured or far away.*

henry thoreau

empathy is humanity

* * * *

*this above all
   to thine own self be true*

*william
shakespeare*

know thyself

delphic oracle

*do not feel superior or inferior
 to any person*

strive for equality

* * * *

*the life which is unexamined
 is not worth living*

socrates

*make sure you are the one
who made the big splash*

it could have been someone behind you

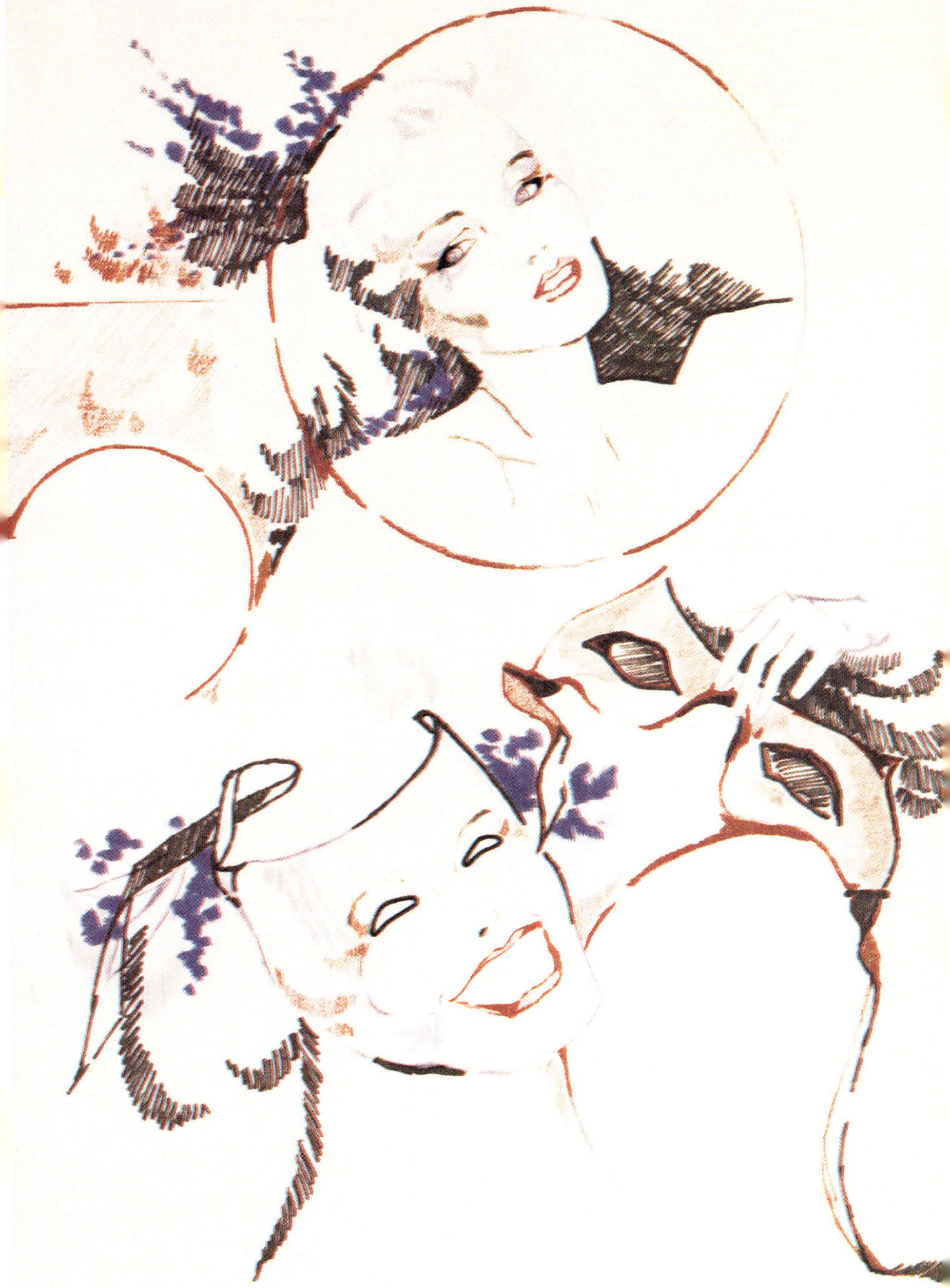

*he who is flat on his back
has no where to go but up*

* * * *

to forget is to forgive

* * * *

*silence
is the element
in which
great things fashion themselves*

thomas carlyle

if you cannot reach
　a life preserver
　　you have gone too far

　　　* * * *

to have,- to hold,- and,- in time,-

　let go

　　　　　laurence hope

　the son
is a refraction of
　the father

　　　* * * *

if you manipulate me
   who pulls the strings
      when you're gone

     * * * *

don't help me so much,-
   support me
don't do it for me,-
   show me
don't tell me what to do,-
   advise me

  just don't go away

     * * * *

to be or not to be
   that is the question

                     william
                       shakespeare

truly yours

if integrity is involved
    I dare not compromise it
if honesty is needed
    I cannot elude it
if loyalty is expected
    I will not deny it, and
if trust is required
    I must not escape it

for the end of man is his
    compatibility with truth

* * * *

*one cannot run like a gazelle
    with the legs of a turtle*

* * * *

*God grant me the serenity
    to accept the things
I cannot change
the courage to change the
    things I can
and the wisdom to know the
    difference*

                              unknown

*reality can still have
    form
        color
            and
                depth*

* * * *

imminently yours

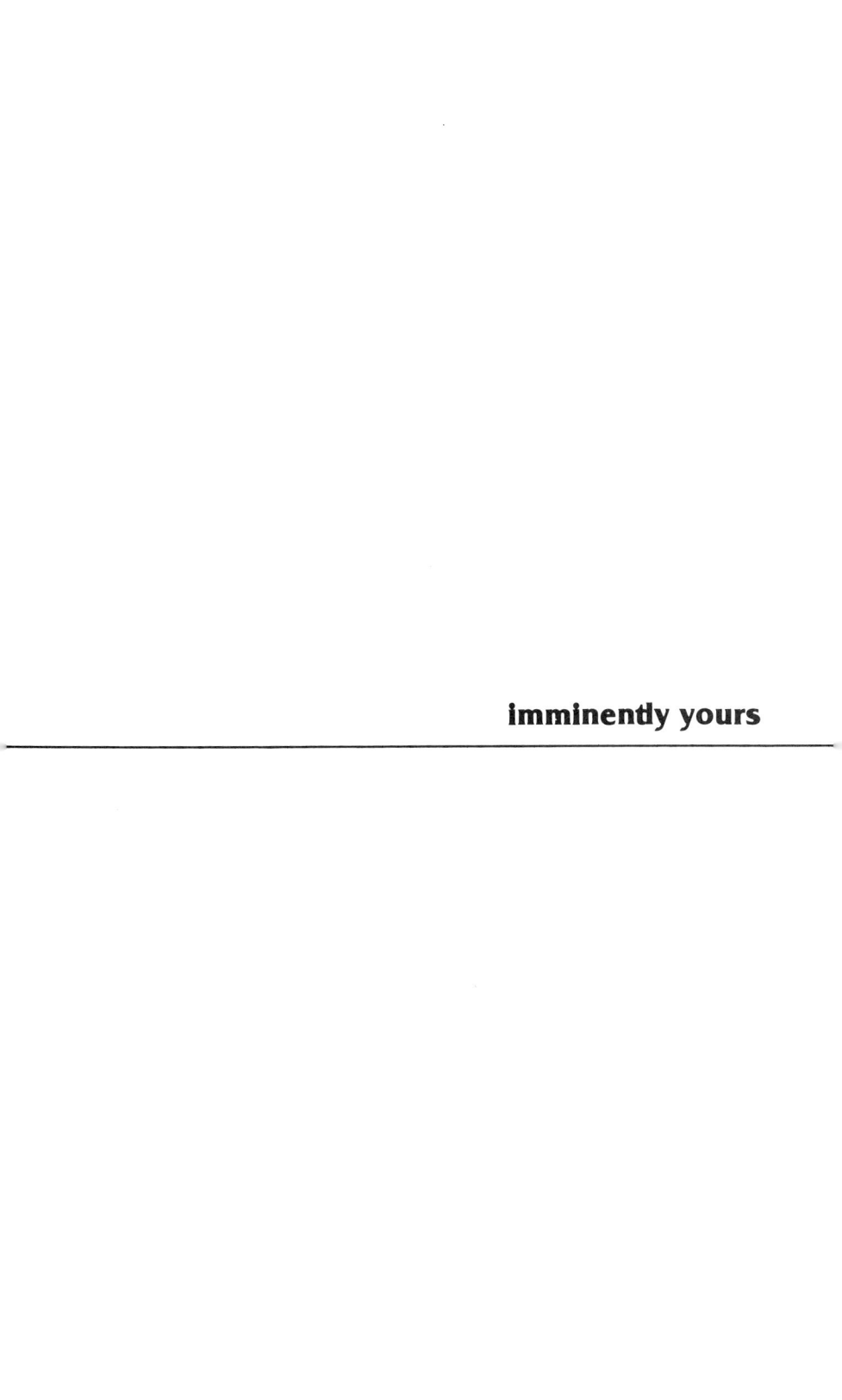

there is no tranquility without anxiety; or happiness without sadness.

there is no mastery without practice; or perfection without error.

there is no independence without dependence; or freedom without controls.

there is no agreement without opposition; or leisure without hard work.

there is no fulfillment without frustration; or escape without concentration,

or love without commitment, or faith without doubt.

for every action has an equal and opposite reaction.

* * * *

when you understand
    you are understood
        and trusted when you trust

when you forgive
    you are forgiven
        and loved when you love

* * * *

to struggle
to test
to listen
to progress
to dissolve and disperse
to emerge,
      victorious

* * * *

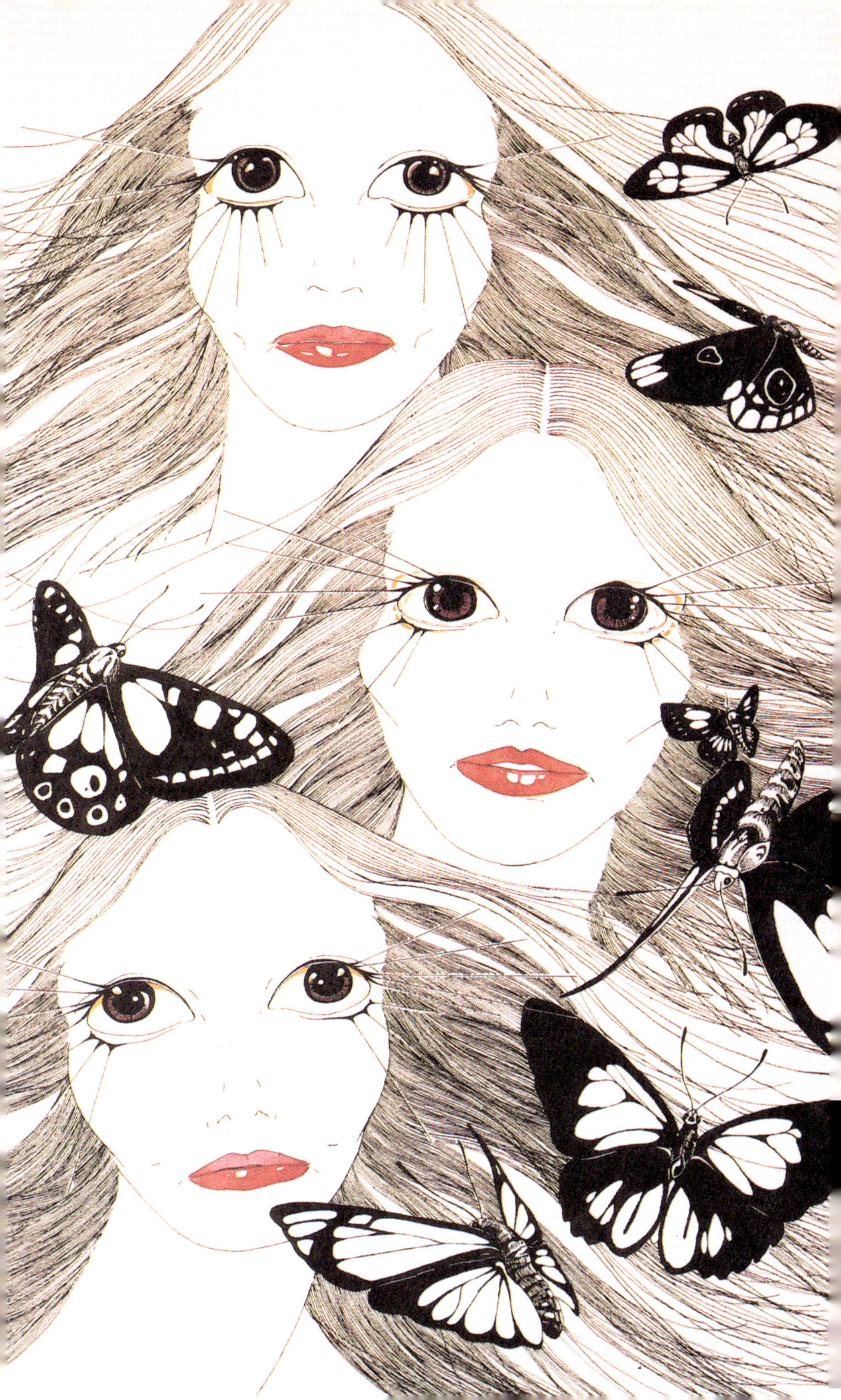

the worth of a person is

*not where you are in this world
   but how you got there*

*not how many successes you've had
   but how you took the failures*

*not in the words you speak
   but in the actions you take*

*not in how many people like you
   but whether you like yourself*

*or, not how many people control you
   but whether you control yourself*

* * * *

*for every thing there is a
season and a proper time is for
every pursuit under the heavens.*

*there is a time to be born and
a time to die; a time to plant and
a time to pluck up what hath been
planted;*

*a time to kill, and a time to
heal, a time to break down and a
time to build up;*

*a time to weep, and a time to
laugh; a time to mourn, and a time
to dance;*

*a time to throw away stones, and
a time to gather up stones; a time
to embrace, and a time to be far
from embracing;*

*a time to seek, and a time to
let things be lost; a time to keep,
and a time to throw away;*

*a time to rend, and a time to
sew; a time to keep silence, and a
time to speak;*

*a time to love, and a time to hate;
a time of war, and a time of peace.*

*Ecclesiastes
III*

simplify

*the distance
between two parents
is directely proportional
to the confusion
of the child*

* * * *

*be sympathetic to the frailities
of your mother and father*

some day they may be yours

* * * *

*the way in which to raise a child is
not to let the tail wag the dog*

* * * *

the darkest hour
*   is that before dawn*

william
hazlitt

we cannot
* play*
*   leapfrog*

* with our lives*

* * * *

you have to believe in happiness
* or happiness never comes*
ah, that's the reason a bird can sing
* on his darkest day he believes*

*   in spring*

douglas
malloch

imminently yours

adversity
 is only an intermezzo

   * * * *

acceptance
 of what has happened is the
first step to overcoming the
 consequences of any misfortune

william
james

cowards die many times
*   before their deaths*
the valiant never taste of
*   death but once*

william
shakespeare

the pride
in breaking a habit
is ultimately more rewarding

than the habit itself

* * * *

when did my power
*   begin controlling me*

* * * *

really yours

when we live a life of pretense, we become hidden from ourselves. we can find ourselves again by sharing our passions, immoralities and aspirations with an interested person.

by making ourselves understood by another, we can understand ourselves. speaking of ourselves to another person lends credibility and reality to our perspective.

* * * *

*adults must learn to subdue the
    illusive fears of their
vestigial child by testing each
    fear with the immediate
external circumstances*

★ ★ ★ ★

*a rational person has learned to
approach life with logic,
realistic thought and systematic
problem solving*

* * * *

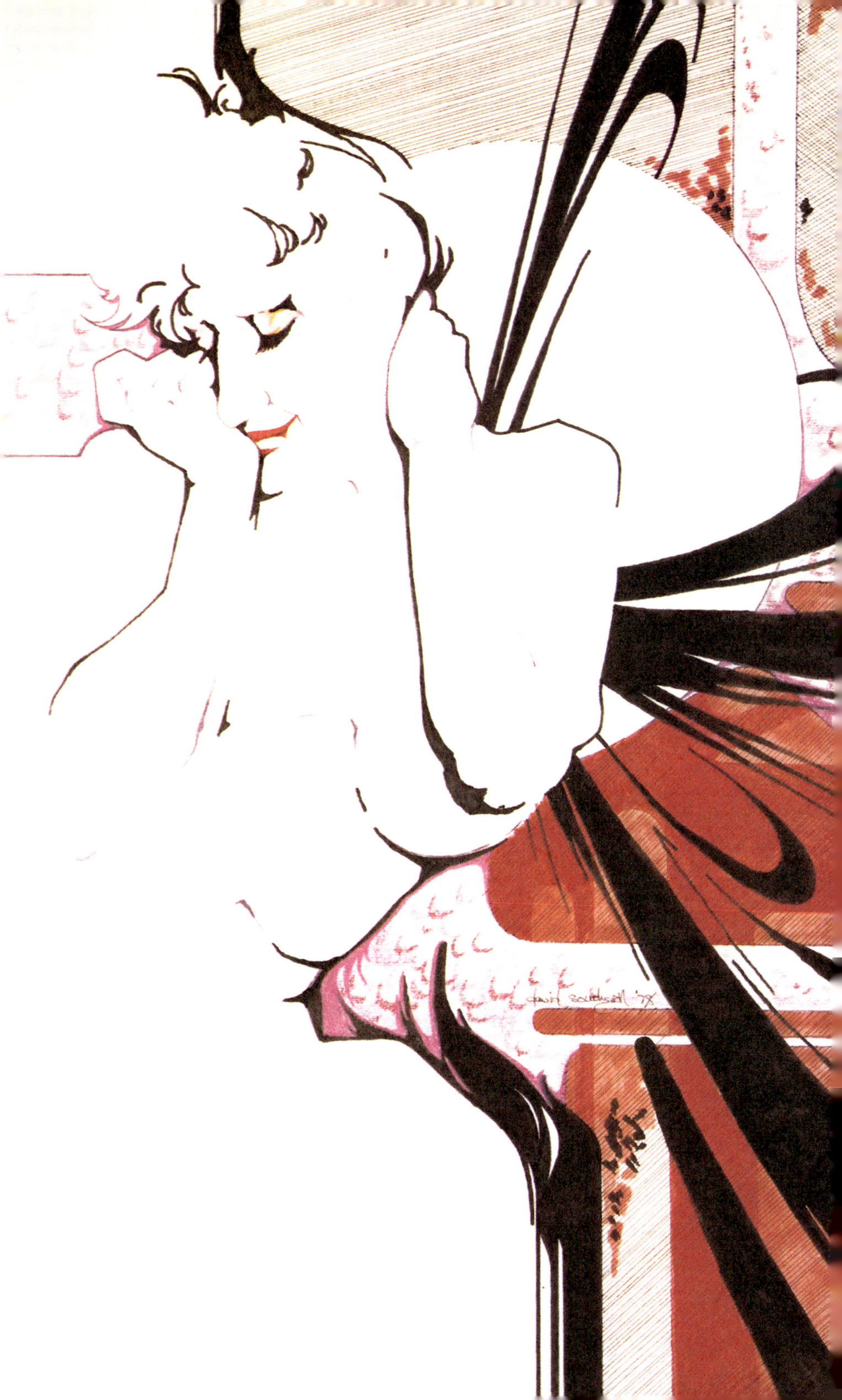

do not set yourself apart from others by considering your failures as unique. you will find comfort in numbers.

* * * *

fulfilled people recognize they receive their sexuality by direct acknowledgment from both parents

* * * *

.

really yours

suffering the unknown by repression of one's emotions is, in the long run, more painful than coping with real feelings.

one must have the courage to feel honest reactions to present moments.

* * * *

mature adults have learned to endure
anxiety until they form a
realistic plan of action. impulsive
behavior and juvenile habits
eases the tension only for the moment
and robs us of exploring
mature, constructive and healthly
outlets.

* * * *

love's condition is a commitment to share your life with another.

love's feeling is secure and comfortable.

love's expression is a life-style reflecting a delicate balance between your needs and those of another.

love is an honest, open relationship, where, for better or for worse, you can be yourself.

* * * *

take care of yourself

sincerely yours,

Jacquie

about the author

Jacquie Hoffman, wife, mother, and humanist, was born and raised in Gary, Indiana. Formerly an executive secretary and paralegal, she has since joined her husband in the operation of their tennis business. The Hoffmans live in Denver, Colorado with their five children.